31 DAILY DEVOTIONS FOR DECEMBER

Tenacity at Christmas

Tenacity at Christmas: 31 Daily Devotions for December
© 2020 by Janet Sketchley

ISBN 978-1-989581-03-2 (print: Prayer Journal Edition)
ISBN 978-1-989581-04-9 (epub)
ISBN 978-1-989581-05-6 (mobi)

All rights reserved, in all media. Brief quotations from the devotional text are permitted in printed or electronic reviews, or on social media if properly attributed to the book and author. Otherwise, no part of this material may be reproduced or transmitted for commercial purposes in any form, without written permission of the author. Scripture quotations are governed by the copyright information below.

Permissions requests may be directed to the author via the contact page on her website: janetsketchley.ca/contact or via email at info@janetsketchley.ca

Scripture quotations marked AMP are taken from the Amplified® Bible (AMP), Copyright © 2015 by The Lockman Foundation. Used by permission. www.Lockman.org

Scripture quotations marked NIV are taken from the Holy Bible, New International Version®, NIV®. Copyright © 1973, 1978, 1984, 2011 by Biblica, Inc.™ Used by permission. All rights reserved worldwide.

Scripture quotations marked NLT are taken from the Holy Bible, New Living Translation, copyright ©1996, 2004, 2015 by Tyndale House Foundation. Used by permission of Tyndale House Publishers, Inc., Carol Stream, Illinois 60188. All rights reserved.

Scripture quotations marked TLB are taken from the Living Bible, copyright © 1971 by Tyndale House Foundation. Used by permission of Tyndale House Publishers Inc., Carol Stream, Illinois 60188. All rights reserved.

Quote from *A Christmas Carol* (December 2: "Incarnation") is from *A Christmas Carol*, by Charles Dickens. Public domain.

Cover by Janet Sketchley. Cover image: iStock.com/Simon Lehmann.
Published in Canada by Janet Sketchley.

RELIGION/ CHRISTIAN LIFE/ DEVOTIONAL/ CHRISTMAS

31 Daily Devotions for December

Tenacity at Christmas

Janet Sketchley
janetsketchley.ca

Foreword

And his name will be the hope of all the world.
Matthew 12:21, NLT

Think about this verse. Isn't it beautiful? Doesn't it cause a quiet peace to well up inside? His Name—Jesus—will be the hope of the whole world.

In your busyness and life circumstances, good or bad...

In your relationships, sweet or strained...

I pray you'll sense His nearness, His gentle hand cradling you, and His love lighting your heart. Because of Jesus, we have hope.

May your Christmas season bring at least one new treasured memory, and may you be blessed to be a blessing.

Janet Sketchley
Canada, 2020

PS: If you're particularly attentive to spelling, you'll notice that the Scripture quotations use US spelling, while my text is Canadian (a hybrid of UK and US). The Bible publishers are US-based, which defines their choice of spelling.

December's journey begins...

Let's read a Bible verse or two and remind ourselves of the Reason for the Season.

December 1

En-Joying Advent

> But the angel said to them, "Do not be afraid. I bring you good news that will cause great joy for all the people.
> Luke 2:10, NIV

Advent—the weeks leading up to Christmas, to the coming of our Saviour King.

It could be a beautiful time of reflection. Worship. Anticipation. Too often these days, it's anything but. And maybe nothing's changed. Not everyone was happy and peaceful in Bethlehem when God broke into human history that first Christmas Day.

In the middle of the frenzy, society has missed the point. It's not about being "ready for Christmas" in the sense of hatches battened down, presents bought and wrapped, cards mailed, freezer stocked with goodies. It's about being contented in Advent. Finding the joy in it and trusting that the other things will come in due time.

Today's responsibility is to choose not to accept the calendar-driven anxiety, but to abide with God and to be alert to His presence. May we also be alert to the gift ideas and other nudges that He will give in His own good time.

Let's take a few quiet minutes each day: hard to carve out of the whirlwind, perhaps, but of great restorative value. Read the Christmas narratives, or some of the Old Testament prophecies of the Messiah. Listen to—truly *hear*—a Christmas carol. Sit with God and ask for His peace.

Precious Saviour, I may not like the commercialism and a lot of what North American culture adds to and subtracts from the observance of Your birth, but please remind me I don't have to beat them or join them. Show me how I can be myself, present with You and enjoying Your presence with me.

Dear Lord,

These are the things I'm concerned about today:

<u>   </u>

<u>   </u>

<u>   </u>

And these are the ways I've seen Your care today:

<u>   </u>

<u>   </u>

<u>   </u>

Help me with

<u>   </u>

<u>   </u>

<u>   </u>

Remind me of

<u>   </u>

<u>   </u>

<u>   </u>

Thank You for loving me.

Amen

December 2

Incarnation

In the beginning was the Word, and the Word was with God, and the Word was God.

The Word became flesh and made his dwelling among us. We have seen his glory, the glory of the one and only Son, who came from the Father, full of grace and truth.
John 1:1,14, NIV

Fully God, fully man... the manger scenes can distract us from this mystery, but in the words of Charles Dickens, "This must be distinctly understood, or nothing wonderful can come of the story I am going to relate" (*A Christmas Carol*, page 1).

We want to see Christmas as a happy, family time, filled with hope and promise, yet we're aware of the pain in the world, the brokenness. But that's why He came.

Can you imagine God choosing to confine Himself to the limitations of a baby... a growing boy... a man? In the squalor and darkness that is our Earth, after dwelling in the glory of Heaven?

He loved us enough to stoop to our level, to look us in the eyes, to carry our pain and punishment so we could be restored to relationship with Him.

Eternal God, Blessed Saviour, Holy Spirit, my mind isn't big enough to grasp the mystery of the Incarnation, but I offer praise and thanks for Jesus, God made flesh, my Deliverer, my King. Thank You for setting Your love on me. Help me receive it, and help me share it.

Dear Lord,

These are the things I'm concerned about today:

_____

_____

_____

And these are the ways I've seen Your care today:

_____

_____

_____

Help me with

_____

_____

_____

Remind me of

_____

_____

_____

Thank You for loving me.

Amen

December 3

Fulfillment

> Praise be to the Lord, the God of Israel,
> because he has come to his people and redeemed them.
> He has raised up a horn of salvation for us
> in the house of his servant David
> (as he said through his holy prophets of long ago).
> Luke 1:68-70, NIV

This is the beginning of Zechariah's song of praise after the birth of his son and the declaration, "His name is John." During his nine (or more!) months of Heaven-sent silence because he hadn't believed the angel Gabriel's message, Zechariah must have had plenty of time to ponder.

Now the Holy Spirit fills him with words, and he pours out this beautiful declaration. It's worth reading in its entirety, verses 68-79, but today let's focus on this: "He has come to his people and redeemed them."

John the Baptist, he who is to prepare the way for the Messiah, has just been born. Jesus Himself won't be born for six more months. He hasn't really "come to His people" yet. He won't go to the Cross and sacrifice Himself for us for another 33 years.

The barest sign of completion has appeared, yet these words of praise declare the work of redemption finished.

That's trust.

God of grace and mercy, when I can't see what You're doing and the wait seems long, please strengthen my faith to count Your work as done. Help me praise You in the waiting and walk each day in trust.

Dear Lord,

These are the things I'm concerned about today:

_____

_____

_____

And these are the ways I've seen Your care today:

_____

_____

_____

Help me with

_____

_____

_____

Remind me of

_____

_____

_____

Thank You for loving me.

Amen

December 4

Preparing for His Coming

Then Moses said, "This is what the LORD has commanded you to do, so that the glory of the LORD may appear to you."
Leviticus 9:6, NIV

There's something about the Scriptures detailing the preparations for God's coming into the Israelites' Tabernacle, with the people freshly under his Law, that makes me wonder about the preparations for Jesus' coming as the Son of Man to fulfill the Law and to inaugurate the rule of Grace.

In the New Testament we see the angel Gabriel's announcement to Mary, and before that to Zechariah about the birth of John the Baptist. But God was planning since the beginning for this moment.

We've heard about the birth of Baby Jesus so many times that we can get kind of blasé about it, especially when we're overwhelmed by the non-faith aspects of preparing for the holidays.

The Old Testament is a good cure for blasé-ness about God. It's a reminder of the mystery of this Unknowable One who reveals Himself to us.

Let's pause this Advent season to remember just Who it is we're preparing to welcome.

Jesus, long-promised Saviour, thank You that I don't have to fall down in fear at the manger because You came to rescue, not to condemn. May Your Holy Spirit draw me to my knees in awe and worship. Let my heart prepare You room.

Dear Lord,

These are the things I'm concerned about today:

_____

_____

_____

And these are the ways I've seen Your care today:

_____

_____

_____

Help me with

_____

_____

_____

Remind me of

_____

_____

_____

Thank You for loving me.

Amen

December 5

Cookies and Mangers

She gave birth to her firstborn son. She wrapped him snugly in strips of cloth and laid him in a manger, because there was no lodging available for them.
Luke 2:7, NLT

Christmas cookies. Decorations. Gifts for each one on our list. Sometimes in the fuss and busyness leading up to celebrating Christmas we get caught up in wanting everything to be perfect—and in the stress that inevitably follows our imperfections.

Think, for a minute, about how messy, dusty, smelly, and just plain unsuitable the Bethlehem stable was as the birthplace of the Saviour of the world.

Some suggest the stable was a blessing to Mary and Joseph, a haven from the noise, overcrowding, and general mayhem of the guest rooms. Maybe so. It definitely made the shepherds' visit easier. But it was hardly "perfect."

Look at what *was* perfect, though: the timing, the fulfillment of the Bethlehem prophecy, the willing mother and surrogate father, God Himself in human form. The symbolism: the Divine in a humble, earthly mess.

Patient and perfect Saviour, please help me discern which elements need my best efforts at excellence and which are "optional extras." And help me trust Your perfect working even when I don't meet my own expectations.

Dear Lord,

These are the things I'm concerned about today:

And these are the ways I've seen Your care today:

Help me with

Remind me of

Thank You for loving me.

Amen

December 6

God and People, Reconciled

The Saviour—yes, the Messiah, the Lord—has been born today in Bethlehem, the city of David!
Luke 2:11, NLT

Nobody was ready. They didn't even know He was coming, especially not that way—as a helpless baby—or in that place and moment.

But He came. God incarnate. Because we'd never be ready without His help.

God with us. Our salvation. Our Redeemer. Our friend. Our hope.

The word "sinners" is out of favour these days, perhaps because it conjures images of pointing fingers and judging tones. But "sin" means anything that separates us from God. Sinners, thus, are those people who are separated from Him.

That means all of us, as long as we're living in our own strength. The only One entitled to point the finger chose instead to take on human form, to identify with us, and to bring us back into relationship with Himself.

God and sinners reconciled.

Not a bad gift at all.

Creator and Redeemer God, I could never earn Your favour, but You love me too much to abandon me when I fall short. As I accept Your great gift of salvation, all I can offer is my heart in obedient trust and love. I am Yours, and I rejoice in Your presence.

Dear Lord,

These are the things I'm concerned about today:

_____

_____

_____

And these are the ways I've seen Your care today:

_____

_____

_____

Help me with

_____

_____

_____

Remind me of

_____

_____

_____

Thank You for loving me.

Amen

December 7

When the Wait is Long

> At that time there was a man in Jerusalem named Simeon. He was righteous and devout and was eagerly waiting for the Messiah to come and rescue Israel. The Holy Spirit was upon him and had revealed to him that he would not die until he had seen the Lord's Messiah.
> Luke 2:25-26, NLT

Jesus' birth ended a period of 400 years of silence from God. The angel Gabriel had brought personal messages to Zechariah and to Mary, and to Simeon in this passage, but these were private revelations. The nation of Israel as a whole heard nothing. Not even a whisper.

400 years. No prophets. No angelic visitors. Silence.

A remnant of Israel had returned from the Babylonian exile and begun to rebuild, as God had promised. He had also promised a Messiah, a King to come who would rule in power and justice and break the people's bondage for good.

Nobody expected the King to suffer and die first.

Nobody expected to wait so long.

Are you waiting today?

God hasn't forgotten, or changed His mind, or discovered He can't do what He promised. He's waiting too, for the best time to unveil what's coming.

Jesus, please pour out Your peace, hope, love, and joy to sustain each of us in the waiting. Help me celebrate Christmas with a full heart, even if I'm still waiting for a word from You. I choose to celebrate, because indeed, the Christ has come.

Dear Lord,

These are the things I'm concerned about today:

_____

_____

_____

And these are the ways I've seen Your care today:

_____

_____

_____

Help me with

_____

_____

_____

Remind me of

_____

_____

_____

Thank You for loving me.

Amen

December 8

Our Magnificat

> Oh, how my soul praises the Lord.
> How my spirit rejoices in God my Savior!
> For he took notice of his lowly servant girl,
> and from now on all generations will call me blessed.
> For the Mighty One is holy,
> and he has done great things for me.
> Luke 1:46-49, NLT

And so begins Mary's song of praise, sometimes called The Magnificat. A spontaneous outburst of joy to the God who has chosen her as a vessel for the impossible.

Mary's full song of praise in Luke 1:46-55 only touches briefly on what God has done for her personally, likely because Elizabeth had just declared it. Instead she proclaims how what God has done for her—choosing her as the mother of the Messiah—is part of what He has done for all of His people.

The gifts He gives us are often for a greater good.

What has He done for you? For me? How might He want to use it in the world around us?

Let's take time somewhere in the busy Christmas season to prayerfully think this through.

Almighty God, You are the Giver of all good gifts. Thank You for the gift of Your Son and the ongoing work of salvation. Thank You for what You have given me. Please help me recognize Your gifts, and may my heart overflow with gratitude and joy. Help me use my gifts for Your glory and for the benefit of those around me.

Dear Lord,

These are the things I'm concerned about today:

_____

_____

_____

And these are the ways I've seen Your care today:

_____

_____

_____

Help me with

_____

_____

_____

Remind me of

_____

_____

_____

Thank You for loving me.

Amen

December 9

Angel Song

> Though he was God,
> he did not think of equality with God
> as something to cling to.
> Instead, he gave up his divine privileges;
> he took the humble position of a slave
> and was born as a human being.
> Philippians 2:6-7a, NLT

No wonder the angels' announcement split the sky and made the shepherds cower in fear. The angels knew what was going on—at least this part of the story. They'd known since Gabriel told Mary that she would conceive the Messiah. They may have known longer.

Among the humans, only Mary and Joseph knew, and Elizabeth and Zechariah.

This huge, astounding, mind-breaking secret: God Himself became an embryo and was born a baby who was fully God and fully human. And somehow still remained God the Father, ruling the universe.

The angels knew. Can you imagine the sheer jubilation of their announcement?

Today, we know. May we take some time to ponder this news that's more than human minds can grasp. May the Holy Spirit reveal this truth to the depths of our beings.

God the Father, God the Son, God the Holy Spirit, what can I say but "thank You"? What can I do but worship You? Please let the magnitude of the Incarnation change me, for Your glory.

Dear Lord,

These are the things I'm concerned about today:

_____

_____

_____

And these are the ways I've seen Your care today:

_____

_____

_____

Help me with

_____

_____

_____

Remind me of

_____

_____

_____

Thank You for loving me.

Amen

December 10

Light in the Darkness

The Light shines on in the darkness, and the darkness did not understand it or overpower it or appropriate it or absorb it [and is unreceptive to it].
John 1:15, AMP

Israel of 2,000 years past was a pretty dark place, much like today. The presence of Jesus—Immanuel, God with us—still makes the difference.

As we pray for the people and situations nearest to our hearts this season, at first the darkness may seem too much. *This* young girl, *that* family, *this* elderly woman and her caregivers... where they're walking may seem unbearable. The needs can overload our spirits as we pray.

Sometimes we demand *why* of God. Other times, our discontent about what He allows says we don't think very highly of His management. Judging God doesn't end well. And discontent is poison.

If that's where you are today, try praying this verse about the Light in the darkness, but be careful to look at the Light with gratitude for His power and hope in His care.

Let's thank God for what He will do in the areas pressing most heavily on our hearts. Instead of being dragged down by the pain, we can choose to trust that whatever His plans are, they're for good. As we pray for things to get better, we can ask for people to be made new and for others to see the difference God makes.

Sovereign and holy God, sometimes instead of fixing things, You re-create or make new. And the new is better. Stronger. Useful in Your hands. You waste nothing. Help me trust You. Show me how to pray in radical gratitude and praise, confidently trusting You. Shine brighter in the darkness, until all can see Your glory.

Dear Lord,

These are the things I'm concerned about today:

_____

_____

_____

And these are the ways I've seen Your care today:

_____

_____

_____

Help me with

_____

_____

_____

Remind me of

_____

_____

_____

Thank You for loving me.

Amen

December 11

On Joy and Interruptions

And there were shepherds living out in the fields nearby, keeping watch over their flocks at night. An angel of the Lord appeared to them, and the glory of the Lord shone around them, and they were terrified.
Luke 2:9, NIV

Overcrowded because of a politician's census, Bethlehem had no time to spare for the Saviour's birth. He came anyway. And during the shepherds' night watch, the angel's message found an eager response.

December is such a busy time of year. We cram an already-full schedule even fuller with extra events and gatherings, and with the unstated pressure to do it all, "because it's Christmas."

But wait. Jesus didn't come to bring expectations and guilt—just the opposite. He didn't come to drive us into debt or anxiety, but to set us free, enrich our spirits, and pour His peace into troubled hearts.

He came to interrupt our everyday lives and give us new life—abundant life. How often do we cling to the mundane instead? If we're not careful, our joy can be brushed aside by agendas as full as the Bethlehem inn.

This year, instead of carrying the weight of the doing, can we cultivate the *being*? Being still with God, daily exploring the richness of Advent. Being open to the interruptions that December brings to our plans. Choosing to enjoy the opportunities to spend time with friends and family. Hearing and celebrating the music of the season. Being with God, even in a crowded store, and listening for His nudges in what gifts to buy for whom.

Jesus, Giver of abundant life, I don't want to miss the joy of Christmas. Help me respond to You like one of the shepherds, in worship, instead of like a sleeping—or grumpy—citizen of Bethlehem.

Dear Lord,

These are the things I'm concerned about today:

_____

_____

_____

And these are the ways I've seen Your care today:

_____

_____

_____

Help me with

_____

_____

_____

Remind me of

_____

_____

_____

Thank You for loving me.

Amen

December 12

The Baby King

In the beginning the Word already existed.
The Word was with God,
and the Word was God.
He existed in the beginning with God.
God created everything through him,
and nothing was created except through him.
The Word gave life to everything that was created,
and his life brought light to everyone.
John 1:1-4, NLT

At Christmas we talk about the Baby Jesus in the manger, but we mustn't be deceived by the outward helplessness of a newborn. He was with the Father and the Spirit in the beginning, one God in three Persons.

Being born in human flesh was new, but He was not new. This was our King, who came into the world to draw us back to Himself. Our Creator, for a time fully dependent on the people He had created.

As we celebrate the birth of the infant who would grow up to become our Saviour, let's remember the power, authority, and majesty that have always belonged to Jesus from the dawn of time.

He who was born King of the Jews, who opened the way for non-Jews as well, is truly worthy of worship. Even as a tiny baby.

Holy and majestic God, thank You for sending Your Son to walk among us and show us how to follow You. Thank You for the teaching, the miracles, the signs of His authority. Thank You for the Cross that showed His love for us and that rescued us from the evil one's hold. The shepherds and the wise men gave what they could. Help me give my heart.

Dear Lord,

These are the things I'm concerned about today:

_____

_____

_____

And these are the ways I've seen Your care today:

_____

_____

_____

Help me with

_____

_____

_____

Remind me of

_____

_____

_____

Thank You for loving me.

Amen

December 13

The Magnitude of God's Plan

And I will put enmity
between you and the woman,
and between your offspring and hers;
he will crush your head,
and you will strike his heel.
Genesis 3:15, NIV

These were God's words to the serpent (Satan) back in the Garden of Eden, thousands of years before Jesus' birth.

Adam and Eve believed the serpent's lies instead of remembering the truth of God's character. They saw what they wanted and took it, even though they knew better. Their beautiful relationship with God was broken, and life was about to get unbearably hard.

But instead of writing them off, God spoke hope for their future race.

Look at the magnitude of His plan. It would take thousands of years, but at the right time He would send His own Son to be born in human flesh to end Satan's tyranny and restore us to intimacy with God.

Here is One we can trust fully and completely. This is way beyond our ability to understand or to see the big picture, but He has it all in hand. That should inspire our worship.

Creator God, my Saviour and Sustainer, I praise You for the magnitude of Your love and Your compassion for the people You created. You didn't want puppets who'd blindly obey. You wanted us to choose You with free will and to trust You. Thank You for Jesus' victory and for the grace You've poured into my life. Help me trust You and live in Your love.

Dear Lord,

These are the things I'm concerned about today:

_____

_____

_____

And these are the ways I've seen Your care today:

_____

_____

_____

Help me with

_____

_____

_____

Remind me of

_____

_____

_____

Thank You for loving me.

Amen

December 14

His Presence

I am the vine; you are the branches. If you remain in me and I in you, you will bear much fruit; apart from me you can do nothing.
John 15:5, NIV

Sometimes in the frenzy of Christmas preparations we can lose our sense of Jesus' presence, but there's no need to fear we've lost Him in the chaos. No need to despair.

Let's step back, just for a minute. Leave the hubbub. Breathe. Consider.

What do we know about Him? How do we know where to "find" Him? Yes, He's always where we are, but maybe the noise is too much.

Think about the boy Jesus in the Temple, surprised His parents didn't know He would be "about His Father's business" (Luke 2:49).

In our day, what sort of activities might He be involved in? Can we rearrange our schedules to invest some time there, even at the expense of leaving some other things undone?

Are there items on our agendas that He might invite us to put aside? Things that are getting in the way of our awareness of Him?

Lord Jesus, I don't want to miss the joy of a close relationship with You. You are my life, my strength, and my song. You are the joy in my journey. Please teach me how to manage the time You give, and how to be quiet in my spirit even when there's chaos all around. Help me anchor and abide in You.

Dear Lord,

These are the things I'm concerned about today:

_____

_____

_____

And these are the ways I've seen Your care today:

_____

_____

_____

Help me with

_____

_____

_____

Remind me of

_____

_____

_____

Thank You for loving me.

Amen

December 15

Love Incarnate

> And I am convinced that nothing can ever separate us from God's love. Neither death nor life, neither angels nor demons, neither our fears for today nor our worries about tomorrow—not even the powers of hell can separate us from God's love.
> Romans 8:38, NLT

God's love... revealed in a squalling infant given to a humble couple to love. Revealed in Christ's willingness to lay aside His heavenly glory (Philippians 2:7) and confine His radiance in a tiny, helpless, human baby.

He left the splendour of heaven and the vastness of His Father's presence to dwell with ordinary, sinful people.

It was a rescue mission to pay the impossible penalty to free us from spiritual slavery and death, but it was also a mercy mission to reveal the Father's love.

As Jesus grew and ministered, He modelled how to live in relationship with God the Father. And He showed the Father's love every time He healed a hurt or taught the way of life. Even His rebukes to those opposing Him showed love—a love that fights lies and injustice. A love that doesn't back down and doesn't quit.

Jesus, precious Saviour, forgive me when I doubt Your love. You showed it clearly at Your birth and then every step to the Cross and beyond. Please root this verse deep in my spirit and help me know with certainty that Your love cradles me. Thank You for this promise that nothing can separate me from You.

Dear Lord,

These are the things I'm concerned about today:

_____

_____

_____

And these are the ways I've seen Your care today:

_____

_____

_____

Help me with

_____

_____

_____

Remind me of

_____

_____

_____

Thank You for loving me.

Amen

December 16

Believing

Blessed is she who has believed that the Lord
would fulfill his promises to her!
Luke 1:45, NIV

The angel Gabriel's message to Mary was a promise that she would conceive and bear the Messiah. The Messiah Himself is key to the fulfillment of many Old Testament promises for which the people of Israel had waited for centuries.

God spoke, and Mary believed.

It's not about "believing harder" to force our will on God. Nor is it about trying to manipulate circumstances to obligate God to act.

It's about following Mary's humble example, choosing to trust and wait and obey. Sometimes it's about "I believe. Help my unbelief" (see Mark 9:24).

Even the believing is a gift from God. Our role as beloved children is to receive.

Gracious God, thank You for the promises You have made—the ones in Your Word to everyone, and the ones You have whispered into my heart. Help me believe You no matter how impossible or unlikely they may look. What You say, You will do, at just the right time and in marvellous ways. You are good, and I will hope in You.

Dear Lord,

These are the things I'm concerned about today:

_____

_____

_____

And these are the ways I've seen Your care today:

_____

_____

_____

Help me with

_____

_____

_____

Remind me of

_____

_____

_____

Thank You for loving me.

Amen

December 17

When We're Bruised

A bruised reed he will not break,
and a smoldering wick he will not snuff out.
In faithfulness he will bring forth justice;
he will not falter or be discouraged
till he establishes justice on earth.
In his teaching the islands will put their hope.
Isaiah 42:3-4, NIV

Sometimes we feel bruised, smouldering, almost extinguished. Whether we're over-stretched by holiday busyness or crushed by circumstances, we have nothing left to give.

Jesus came for these times, into a world in that state even if its people didn't recognize their need. Our gentle Shepherd knows our weakness and will carry us in His compassion.

The justice Isaiah promises may not be seen fully in this life, but it's coming. And the biggest component of that justice, ultimately the most important, is making us right again with God. Of that part, Jesus said "It is finished."

Dear God, Your compassion never ends and Your love never fails. Please remind me of Your tender care. Help me trust You to carry me when I'm weak and to work in my life and in my loved ones according to Your mercy.

Dear Lord,

These are the things I'm concerned about today:

———————————————————————————
———————————————————————————
———————————————————————————

And these are the ways I've seen Your care today:

———————————————————————————
———————————————————————————
———————————————————————————

Help me with

———————————————————————————
———————————————————————————
———————————————————————————

Remind me of

———————————————————————————
———————————————————————————
———————————————————————————

Thank You for loving me.

Amen

December 18

Hope is Born

For to us a child is born,
to us a son is given,
and the government will be on his shoulders.
And he will be called
Wonderful Counselor, Mighty God,
Everlasting Father, Prince of Peace.
Isaiah 9:6, NIV

Jesus left the glory of heaven to be born as a human child and began the fulfillment of God's redemption promise from Genesis.

Imagine setting aside His rightful glory as God, submitting to the indignity of birth and infancy, to human frailty, rustic conditions and death... to redeem us. Not because He had to, but because He chose to out of love.

The world is still dark and painful. But if we're open, He does bring wholeness. Hope. Circumstances may not change, but He came to be God with us. We don't have to do this alone.

Somehow His grace gives us strength, His wisdom leads us, His love in our hearts warms us. Because we trust Him, we can say "though I walk through the darkest valley, I will fear no evil..." (Psalm 23:4, NIV).

Christmas is a hard time for people who are hurting, because the world puts on its happy mask and avoids them. But Jesus' birth affirms the pain. That's why He came.

Father, how can I help but love and praise You for reaching into our world's mess to bring hope and healing? This Christmas season may I celebrate Your greatest gift, may Your love flow through me to those I touch, and may the world in its turmoil somehow pause to receive its King. Thank You that someday every knee will bow and every tongue confess Jesus as Lord. Until then, have mercy on us all.

Dear Lord,

These are the things I'm concerned about today:

_____

_____

_____

And these are the ways I've seen Your care today:

_____

_____

_____

Help me with

_____

_____

_____

Remind me of

_____

_____

_____

Thank You for loving me.

Amen

December 19

Quiet Trust

"I am the Lord's servant," Mary answered. "May your word to me be fulfilled." Then the angel left her.
Luke 1:38, NIV

The angel said Mary would conceive when "The Holy Spirit will come on you, and the power of the Most High will overshadow you" (Luke 1:35, NIV).

That wasn't a lot of detail for her to wrap her head around. But he also gave her the news of Elizabeth's miracle as something to hold onto.

Mary knew the prophecies and expectations of the Messiah. Like the other Jewish girls, she probably dreamed of being the Chosen One's mother. But she wasn't married yet and clearly understood that Gabriel wasn't talking about waiting for a wedding.

He was talking about *very soon*. If she had presence of mind to think this through while talking with an angel, she'd be aware of the risk and shame that came with being an unwed mother in those days.

Still, Mary said yes. Her trust, love, and obedience to God were greater than her need to understand or to play it safe. She may not have known much about the how, but she believed God.

Holy God, Your ways are beyond our understanding, and You use the small and weak to show Your magnitude and strength. When I think of who You are, my spirit responds in worship. Please open me to hear You, and give me grace to trust, love, and obey You even when I don't understand the bigger picture.

Dear Lord,

These are the things I'm concerned about today:

_____

_____

_____

And these are the ways I've seen Your care today:

_____

_____

_____

Help me with

_____

_____

_____

Remind me of

_____

_____

_____

Thank You for loving me.

Amen

December 20

A Perfect Fit

For God so loved the world that he gave his one and only Son, that whoever believes in him shall not perish but have eternal life.
John 3:16, NIV

The best gifts are the ones we don't see coming, the ones we don't know we've longed for or needed until they're there in our hands, surprising and delighting some deep part of our souls. We cry, "It's perfect!"

From then on, even the thought of the gift warms our hearts and makes us brim with love and gratitude to the giver.

God gave us Jesus. A perfect fit—a perfect fix for the brokenness that is life separated from God. To a lost, confused, and dying world, He gave light. Hope. Himself. And the Bible is clear that God planned this gift from the beginning. It was His initiative, not ours.

In the preparations to celebrate Jesus' birth, in the whirl of activities and gatherings, let's pause to remember the Gift we've received—the Gift we can carry with us every crowded minute of each day.

Precious Father, what kind of love is this that gives so lavishly to those who can never repay You? In Jesus You've given me exactly what my soul needs most. You've saved me from the curse of sin and death and adopted me as Your treasured child. In Your embrace I find wholeness and peace. I find my true self. There are no words to thank You, God. Help me thank You by embracing Your Son and living wholeheartedly in His light.

Dear Lord,

These are the things I'm concerned about today:

And these are the ways I've seen Your care today:

Help me with

Remind me of

Thank You for loving me.

Amen

December 21

God Has Heard Your Prayer

But the angel said, "Don't be afraid, Zechariah! God has heard your prayer. Your wife, Elizabeth, will give you a son, and you are to name him John."
Luke 1:13, NLT

By this time Zechariah and Elizabeth were very old. In their culture, imagine the whispers that must have swirled for years, part pity and part judgement. What did they do wrong? What secret sin kept Elizabeth barren? (Somehow it never seemed to be a problem on the man's side!) What was wrong with Zechariah's faith—and him a priest, at that?

This late in life, was he still praying for a son? Or had he given up?

Yet God had planned for this moment all along. This baby announcement was far more than just answering a childless couple's plea—God was involving them in His story.

What are you waiting for? Praying for?

Will you love God even if He says no? Are you open to Him saying "yes, and here's more" when He knows the time is right?

God Who Hears, You know the cry of my heart. In Your Word I see Your power, Your love, and Your compassion. Once again I give You my request. I don't know what You plan, or when, but I believe that Your way is best. In the words of Jesus, "Not my will but Thine be done." Help me wait in trust and in confidence in Your goodness.

Dear Lord,

These are the things I'm concerned about today:

_____

_____

_____

And these are the ways I've seen Your care today:

_____

_____

_____

Help me with

_____

_____

_____

Remind me of

_____

_____

_____

Thank You for loving me.

Amen

December 22

This is the LORD's Battle

This is what the LORD says: Do not be afraid! Don't be discouraged by this mighty army, for the battle is not yours, but God's.
2 Chronicles 20:15b, NLT

In today's verse, God made it clear that it wasn't up to the people to achieve the victory. They were to act in trust and obedience to Him.

What does this have to do with Christmas?

While our preparations shouldn't feel like a battle—although they can at times—the pressures do mount, the calendar is counting down, and we often take on too much responsibility. We're bearing a burden of ownership that God never intended.

Are there ways to simplify? Are we carrying things we've placed on our own shoulders that aren't necessary? Or are we doing things that others expect when we may need to prayerfully and gently set boundaries?

Whatever we're doing, no matter how important, let's remember the battle is the Lord's. We're not in control. We're not the boss, nor the victor. But He is. What He has allowed into our lives for us to do, areas for us to serve in our communities, our churches, workplaces, and families, He gives the strength and the equipping to complete.

Can we rest and rely on Him and experience serving without stressing?

Holy and strong God, thank You that where You call, You equip. You are my sufficiency and my competence. Please show me where to focus my attention today and each day of this blessed Christmas season. Don't let me miss the joy by taking on responsibility for getting everything done or making everything perfect. Lead me in what to do, and help me trust You to bring it all together. Thank You for Your mercy and grace.

Dear Lord,

These are the things I'm concerned about today:

_____

_____

_____

And these are the ways I've seen Your care today:

_____

_____

_____

Help me with

_____

_____

_____

Remind me of

_____

_____

_____

Thank You for loving me.

Amen

December 23
At the Right Time

> But when the right time came, God sent his Son, born of a woman, subject to the law. God sent him to buy freedom for us who were slaves to the law, so that he could adopt us as his very own children.
> Galatians 4:4-5, NLT

Way back in the Book of Genesis, when sin first separated us from Him, God promised a Saviour (Genesis 3:15). Years passed. People lived and died. Life was hard.

The Bible speaks of promises fulfilled after many years, and promises still waiting their time. Christmas is part of what makes the believing and the waiting possible.

How should we conduct ourselves in the waiting?

Let's consciously practice His presence, learning to abide with Him like sheep with their shepherd. Let's cultivate a heart-posture of conscious submission, adoration, and trust.

God did send His Son into the world as our Messiah. He does keep His promises.

Holy and mighty Lord God, my time is not Your time, nor my understanding Yours. You know the short length of my life, and You remember the promises You have for me. Help me trust You and wait in obedience and peace, not fretting and chafing, not fearing that You'll fail me. You are a promise-keeping God, and I love You.

Dear Lord,

These are the things I'm concerned about today:

And these are the ways I've seen Your care today:

Help me with

Remind me of

Thank You for loving me.

Amen

December 24

Trusting God

While they were there, the time came for the baby to be born, and she gave birth to her firstborn, a son. She wrapped him in cloths and placed him in a manger, because there was no guest room available for them.
Luke 2:6-7, NIV

A ruler's whim forced a very pregnant Mary to travel to Bethlehem for a census. Can you imagine how uncomfortable a donkey-ride that was?

When she and Joseph finally found a place to stay, it was a stable. Small, cramped, maybe with a low roof. Some scholars suggest it was a cave, not a wooden building. Hay-dust would have hung in the air. So would the smell of animals—not necessarily clean animals.

Mary had never given birth. Here she was, away from home and all the support of family, in a strange and inappropriate place. But she didn't panic, freak out, or dissolve in a poor-me pity party. She didn't ask God where He was and why He wasn't looking after her—and looking after His Child.

She trusted God. With the angel's words in her memory, along with every other experience she had of God's care, her faith remained secure. And she made the best of her situation.

May we do the same.

God Most High, You could have provided a palace for Your Son's birth, but You chose to send Him to us in obscurity. There's a lot of symbolism in Jesus' birth and in the choices You made in who to invite to greet Him. Mary wouldn't have known that, and yet she trusted Your care. Please help me to remember her example, and to think of how You've cared for me in the past. Please help me trust You in the present, in the easy and the hard. And show me how to live by faith, whatever my circumstances.

Dear Lord,

These are the things I'm concerned about today:

And these are the ways I've seen Your care today:

Help me with

Remind me of

Thank You for loving me.

Amen

December 25

God's Gift

Though he was God,
he did not think of equality with God
as something to cling to.
Instead, he gave up his divine privileges;
he took the humble position of a slave
and was born as a human being.
Philippians 2:6-7a, NLT

Jesus emptied Himself and took on the form of a human. He didn't even come as an adult, but chose to begin as a developing embryo and be born completely dependent on human parents.

He came to die for us as a ransom, but first to teach truth and to model how a human can live with God in trusting obedience. He came to lead us into relationship with God and to show the Father's heart.

What a gift God has given us—undeserved, unearned, unimaginable. God the Son set aside the fullness of His nature and squeezed into the messy, limited, powerless form of a baby. For us.

He loves us this much.

Jesus, what can I do but praise You and fall on my face before You? Your extravagant love undoes me. It rescues me. It repurposes me. Help me give my whole heart to You, holding nothing back—just as You held nothing back for me.

Dear Lord,

These are the things I'm concerned about today:

_____

_____

_____

And these are the ways I've seen Your care today:

_____

_____

_____

Help me with

_____

_____

_____

Remind me of

_____

_____

_____

Thank You for loving me.

Amen

December 26

Wonder and Trust

All who heard the shepherds' story were astonished, but Mary kept all these things in her heart and thought about them often.
Luke 2:18-19, NLT

The shepherds saw wonders. Mary herself saw wonders! She held the Wonder of the world in her arms.

Do you think what she experienced in Bethlehem helped her keep hoping in the difficult days ahead? Surely it helped her worship this God who loved and chose her. She'd already seen Him provide, and she knew He wouldn't abandon her and Joseph now.

Let's be encouraged and inspired by Mary's humble sense of obedience and trust. Let's consciously keep in our hearts those precious times we've seen God touch our lives, and think about them often.

Maybe as we begin a new year it's time to start (or re-start) a journal for gratitude or to track answered prayer. Or perhaps it's time for a fresh commitment to keep watch for "God moments" in our days.

Precious, loving God, You are so kind in the ways You involve Yourself in my daily life. Whether it's something major like Your call on Mary's life or something as simple as helping me find a lost item, please help me recognize Your care. Help me keep these things in my own heart and think about them often, especially when the times of trouble come. May my spirit be kept in Your perfect peace because I know I can trust in You.

Dear Lord,

These are the things I'm concerned about today:

_____

_____

_____

And these are the ways I've seen Your care today:

_____

_____

_____

Help me with

_____

_____

_____

Remind me of

_____

_____

_____

Thank You for loving me.

Amen

December 27

No "Plan B"

...in the Lamb's book of life, the Lamb who was slain from the creation of the world.
Revelation 13:8b, NIV

Jesus' birth wasn't a "plan B" to salvage creation gone awry. It was an integral part of God's plan before the first atom was spoken into place.

He made us even though He knew what it would cost to redeem us. God loves and desires us that much!

As we move into a new year, fresh from celebrating the wonder of His gift to us in the Incarnation, as we progress toward Easter and the celebration of our King who conquered death for us, let us go with confidence in the God whose purposes never fail and whose heart is always true. Nothing is too hard for Him.

Scripture promises that our "times are in His hands" (Psalm 31:15). He has shown us that He loves us and that He's trustworthy. May we live in this hope.

Dear Jesus, thank You for a love that's more than I can comprehend. For all You've done, I worship You and I give You my heart in love. Teach me to walk with You and to rejoice in Your good care. Free me from any fear and anxiety over the future, and help me live in confident trust in You.

Dear Lord,

These are the things I'm concerned about today:

_____

_____

_____

And these are the ways I've seen Your care today:

_____

_____

_____

Help me with

_____

_____

_____

Remind me of

_____

_____

_____

Thank You for loving me.

Amen

December 28

Waiting Quietly

Let all that I am wait quietly before God,
for my hope is in him.
Psalm 62:5, NLT

Leading up to Christmas Day, children wait, but it's not quietly even if they're silent. Anticipation thrums beneath the surface, reveals itself in twitches and fidgets and jostling.

In these days at the end of December, when we've celebrated the Hope and Light of the World born in Bethlehem, when we've perhaps run ourselves ragged to be ready to receive Him, there's a different kind of waiting.

Let it be a holy hush, a waiting before Him to refresh our souls. An acceptance of His invitation to "Come to me, all of you who are weary and carry heavy burdens, and I will give you rest" (Matthew 11:28, NLT).

Let it be a time of quieting our souls before Him and listening for what He may say to lead us into the new year.

Jesus, Master and Shepherd, You are my light and my hope. Thank You for Your good care. Please quiet me in Your presence and help me find rest in You. Is there something You want to say to me here in the stillness? Open my ears to hear, and my heart to receive.

Dear Lord,

These are the things I'm concerned about today:

_____

_____

_____

And these are the ways I've seen Your care today:

_____

_____

_____

Help me with

_____

_____

_____

Remind me of

_____

_____

_____

Thank You for loving me.

Amen

December 29

Held Secure

My times are in your hands.
Psalm 31:15a, NIV

In this psalm David was crying out to God for protection from his enemies, but this little phrase can speak peace to us whatever our circumstances.

Not that we're to sit back and do nothing, or to become fatalistic and glum. Knowing that God holds us—if we truly trust His character—gives the confidence we need to live each day with hope.

He's got this—whatever *this* is. It may be bigger than we are, but it's not bigger than God. It may be more than we can figure out, but it's not beyond His wisdom. It may even be meant for harm, but He can use it for good (see Romans 8:28).

We can be almost guaranteed His ways won't be our ways, His answers not the ones we ask for. But we have His promise to care for us, and His word is true.

Nothing will surprise Him or catch Him off-guard. Nothing will stump Him or defeat Him. He knows the plans He has for us, and they are good.

Sovereign God, thank You for giving me life, and for what this next year holds. You are good, and You cradle me in Your strong and gentle hands, so please help me trust You completely. Speak peace anytime fear rises up, and remind me that You work all things—the best and the worst—for good in the lives of those who trust You. Help me learn to rest securely in Your love.

Dear Lord,

These are the things I'm concerned about today:

_____

_____

_____

And these are the ways I've seen Your care today:

_____

_____

_____

Help me with

_____

_____

_____

Remind me of

_____

_____

_____

Thank You for loving me.

Amen

December 30

Questions and Promises

Zechariah said to the angel, "How can I be sure this will happen? I'm an old man now, and my wife is also well along in years."

Mary asked the angel, "But how can this happen? I am a virgin."
Luke 1:18, 34, NLT

Zechariah's doubting question left him unable to speak until John was born, and although it was a rebuke it gave him a physical confirmation to hold onto. Mary's practical question brought her a practical, if somewhat hard to envision, answer.

In both cases the hearers submitted to God with as much faith as they had, and God worked through them.

We may or may not have a specific promise from the Lord—one that seems a long time in coming, or that looks impossible to human eyes.

We do have His promises in the Bible: Jesus will never leave us. If we confess our sins, He will forgive and cleanse us. If we trust Him when we ask for wisdom, He will give it. And many more.

When we have questions, when we don't see how things will unfold, we can bring them to God. After all, He knows our hearts. But let's remember to ask in trust, not in doubt or fear.

May we learn to take God at His Word as we move into the unknown of a new year, even when we need to ask Him to help our unbelief.

Promise-keeping God, You have revealed Yourself in so many ways and yet I still sometimes need reassurance. Thank You for Your compassion and for Your mercy that accepts me in my weakness and offers the faith and the forgiveness I need. You are worthy of all praise and worship, and You are so kind to me. Please help me grow in faith and trust, and help me truly believe what You say.

Dear Lord,

These are the things I'm concerned about today:

And these are the ways I've seen Your care today:

Help me with

Remind me of

Thank You for loving me.

Amen

December 31

Into the New Year

And now just as you trusted Christ to save you, trust him, too, for each day's problems; live in vital union with him. Let your roots grow down into him and draw up nourishment from him. See that you go on growing in the Lord, and become strong and vigorous in the truth you were taught. Let your lives overflow with joy and thanksgiving for all he has done.
Colossians 2: 6-7, TLB

Don't you love this encouragement from Paul that we can trust Jesus for each day's problems? Whatever happens, Jesus will be with us. He promised.

We've come to the finish of the in-between days after Christmas Day and before the new year begins. For many, this means a return to "normal," with crowded schedules and long to-do lists.

In the regular routines of life, and in the prayers of our hearts, let's remember and consciously choose to remain... to abide... to find our Source in Him. As a broken-off branch withers and dies, we lose our effectiveness if we allow ourselves to be distracted (John 15:5).

May we seize quiet moments with the Lord, to root in Him and draw nourishment from Him. To grow in the truth we've been taught.

Lord Jesus, thank You for giving me ears to hear about You and faith to believe. Please help me be intentional about growing in my relationship with You. Help me live in vital union with You, and teach me to overflow with gratitude and joy because of what You've done. Thank You, too, for what You will do in the year ahead.

Dear Lord,

These are the things I'm concerned about today:

_____

_____

_____

And these are the ways I've seen Your care today:

_____

_____

_____

Help me with

_____

_____

_____

Remind me of

_____

_____

_____

Thank You for loving me.

Amen

Notes

Notes

Author's Note

Thank you for taking this journey through the Scriptures with me, and I pray the Lord has used this time to bless you this month. All the best in the new year!

If you've found these devotions helpful, take a look at my 365-day devotional, *A Year of Tenacity*. Available in print as well as ebook, it's not tied to calendar dates like this December one so if you miss a day or two you there's no catch-up—just continue on! Please note, the print version doesn't have prayer journal pages like this book.

Also, if you've appreciated this little book, please share it with your friends and consider leaving a review at Goodreads.com and/or at your favourite online store. Reviews help other readers find more books to love.

Thank you to Ruth Ann Adams, Heidi Newell, and Beverlee Wamboldt for their sharp-eyed proofreading, and to my local writers' group for their input in the book description. Any mistakes are due to things I've adjusted after the fact.

I'm predominantly a fiction writer, but devotionals were a labour of love on my blog, *Tenacity*, for many years. If you enjoy Christian fiction, I invite you to check out my novels, listed on the next page. And if you're on Bookbub, I invite you to follow me at bookbub.com/authors/janet-sketchley.

Blessings,
Janet

PS: I hope the contrast between American spelling in the Scripture quotes and Canadian in the devotional text wasn't too jarring. Bible publishers don't make Canadian versions for some reason, and I feel strongly about not giving up my native spelling.

Also by Janet Sketchley

The Redemption's Edge Series:

Heaven's Prey

Secrets and Lies

Without Proof

The Green Dory Inn Mysteries:

Unknown Enemy

Hidden Secrets

Bitter Truth

Deadly Burden

Nonfiction:

A Year of Tenacity
365 Daily Devotions to Warm Your Spirit and Encourage Your Heart

Reads to Remember
A book lover's journal to track your next 100 reads
(paperback only, available with two cover choices)

About the Author

 Janet Sketchley crafts clean, faith-filled mysteries and suspense with characters who feel like friends. She's also the author of two books of daily devotionals for Christian women, and the creator of a journal to track your next 100 reads. Janet writes in Atlantic Canada, where many of her books are set.

You can find Janet online at janetsketchley.ca, and you're invited to subscribe to her newsletter at <u>janetsketchley.ca/subscribe</u> or follow her on BookBub.

www.ingramcontent.com/pod-product-compliance
Lightning Source LLC
Chambersburg PA
CBHW051349040426
42453CB00007B/491